Oh Africa
My Africa

NANCY H. SWEET

MHS AACC
PUBLISHERS

OH AFRICA
MY AFRICA

A Personal Encounter With The Ghanaian People
And The Culture Of Africa

NANCY H. SWEET

MARCUS HORTON SWEET
AFRICAN-AMERICAN CULTURE CENTER

ISBN 0-9640134-0-1
Library of Congress Catalog Card Number 93-91845

Published by
The Marcus Horton Sweet African-American Culture Center
Box 41
Malvern, Pennsylvania 19355-2482 USA
610/647-3302

Second edition, first printing: March 1994
First edition, first printing: October 1992

OH AFRICA
MY AFRICA

A Personal Encounter With The Ghanaian People
And The Culture Of Africa

Contents

Acknowledgments 9

Preface 11

Introduction 13

Foreword 15

Dedication 17

Section One 19

1 *A New Beginning* 21

2 *The Pyramids and the Sphinx* 23

3 *Arrival in Accra, Ghana* 25

Section Two 27

4 *Day One in Accra, Ghana* 29

5 *Grandma Alice's Orphanage Home* 31

6 *The Reburial of Dr. DuBois* 33

7 *Kumasi* 35

Section Three 39

8 *Downtown Accra: The Investment Centre* 41

9 *The City Hall of Accra* 43

10 *Ghana Institute of Journalism* 47

11 *The Art Center* 51

12 *The Mayor's Residence* 53

Section Four 55

13 *The Castles of Cape Coast* 57

14 *Time Out* 63

15 *The Village of Aburi* 67

Section Five 71

16 *Hospitality, Akbar Style* 73

17 *Ghana Beaches* 75

Section Six 77

18 *Farewell to Ghana* 79

19 *Reflections* 81

Notes 83

Glossary 85

Recommended Readings 87

Nancy H. Sweet Biographical Sketch 89

Typesetting: Lauralynn Sweet

Utility: Laser-driven CorelVentura Publisher for Windows ™ version 4.2

Acknowledgments

Compiling information and pictures for this book was made relatively easy because of the cooperation of many of the people who were on the "Adventure in Ghana" tour of 1991. The tour is one of several that have been sponsored by Minister Akbar Muhammad and his wife and children, Sister Maryam, Samimah, Samaiyah, and Lateefah.

Minister Akbar is the International Representative for the Nation of Islam, so acknowledgment is duly made for the help of many Ghanaian government officials through his efforts and contacts.

Reverend P.L. Hailey, Jr., my pastor at Shorter AME Church, Morton, PA, gets a special "thank you" for his provocative and inspiring foreward. James Spady, of Philadelphia, offered me advice.

Help from my family members was encouraging. Sarah, my elder daughter, painted the original artwork for the cover. Patrick, my youngest son, wrote the introduction. Lauralynn, my youngest, typed, edited, and proof-read the book, and designed and created the lay-out for both the book and the cover. To all of these, I am grateful.

Preface

To know oneself is beautifully illustrated in the Holy Scriptures. Equipped with self-knowledge, I am able to rise above the confusion of who I am, and claim my rightful position-place-among the first beings that God created from the banks of the river.

Oh Africa, My Africa , my first encounter with my people, is the missing link that makes me whole. Here, I come face to face and heart to heart with those who invented the tools and mastered the knowledge that shaped society.

Through these pages, travel with me through twelve days of enlightenment, mixed with happiness, sadness, frustration, joy, stress; feel my passion, my true sense of belonging. Kneel with me at the feet of Chief Nii Amugi of Accra, Ghana, as I sip spirits from his personal cup as a means of acknowledging the symbolic welcome-mat evoking the blessings of his land, your land, my land, upon the group. Walk with me through the Tema textile factory and witness the transformation of raw cotton into beautiful bolts of cloth. Sit with me in the home of eighty-year old Grandma Alice, founder and director of the SOS Children's Orphanage. Frolic and collect shells on the gentle beaches of Accra.

Listen to the inspiring words of Dr. Ben-Abdallah, the Minister of Culture of Ghana, at the reburial and final resting place of Dr. W.E.B. duBois. Shed tears with me as I stand within the dungeon walls of the castles, where the African captives, not yet slaves, were held hopelessly awaiting the arrival of the cargo-not passenger- ship, that would take them across the Atlantic Ocean to the inhumane system of slavery. Standing in the dungeon with its small opening, a ray of sunlight paused on a sister's cheek, creating a rainbow on her face: I was reminded of Noah, when God placed a rainbow in the sky, symbolizing freedom, the ends of the rains.

Several myths are dispelled, and credibility is given to the very essence of our being. Although a thousand miles removed, and hundreds of years changed, my people still remain the product of a rich and glorious society.

None can take that inheritance from us.

Nancy H. Sweet
25 November 1993

Introduction

Oh Africa, My Africa is an outline of an African-American woman's journey through the African countries of Egypt and Ghana. The term "outline" is used only for lack of a better word, for this work is truly hard to categorize, which is indicative of good pieces of literature.

The perspective of the writer, a retired schoolteacher, adds a refreshing flavor to the manuscript. **Oh Africa, My Africa** can best be described as a detailed journal. The author, while well educated, is not a pure academic not a professional travel critic which eliminates much of the unnecessary pretense that often plagues national magazines' descriptions and accounts of foreign countries.

As you travel with Mrs. Sweet through Egypt and Ghana her enthusiasm for the surroundings is obvious. She describes, with picturesque wonder, the Great Pyramids, the Mighty Sphinx and the sense of timelessness they impart upon those fortunate enough to view them. As she takes her readers from Cairo (Egypt) to Accra (Ghana), Mrs. Sweet's true sense of purpose becomes more and more apparent. This trip was not made merely for sightseeing; it becomes clear that this trip and the subsequent journal were organized to stress the importance of thinking of Africa as a Homeland and a Birthplace.

Mrs. Sweet and her group met and conversed with Tribal Chiefs, Ambassadors, Heads of States, Ministers of Culture, and the Mayor who all stressed the need for African-Americans to link themselves, economically and socially, with Africa; for Africa is indeed the Mother for a great and mighty race.

While it may be true that many of Africa's sons and daughters have been flung to the corners of the globe through means which cannot be described in charitable terms, we as African-Americans should not and cannot ever forget from whence we came.

Mrs. Sweet's work is filled with many inspiring images that reflect the grandeur and majesty of African civilizations. However, these images are tempered by the theme that Africa exists in a dynamic world which is constantly progressing.

We should not view Africa as a quaint testament to a long-past golden age, but as a continent with enormous potential that is ready, willing, and able to compete in the global arena socially, culturally, and economically. Mrs. Sweet is asking us to wake up and look to our folk on that large continent to the east...AFRICA.

Patrick V. Sweet
Unit Head
Delaware Valley Financial Services

Foreword

The significance of life can best be realized through the monitoring of human events. Man's inhumanity to man and his subsequent struggle to right all the wrongs of his environment are the residual effects of man's fall from divine grace and his struggle to be redeemed fully to God's original purpose. But redemption (salvation) can only come when history-ie "HIS" (man's) STORY- is chronicled without the influence of political and/or social prejudices. The story (history) must be told in the full sunlight of truth and honesty.

One way to get to that unequivocal truth and honesty is to tread the sands of past times and listen to the story it tells. Someone has suggested that one cannot adequately comprehend the reality of another unless he is able to walk a mile in the other's shoes. To extricate one self from his own subjectivity and be able to see the "big picture" of life is a difficult task indeed. Yet, thanks to man's God-given gifts of mind and reason, it is possible when pursued with genuine interest and effort.

As a result of the efforts of great historical figures like J.A. Rogers, W.E.B.DuBois, Lerone Bennett Jr. and Benjamin Quarles (to name but a few), I became acquainted with the "big picture" in terms of my relationship to life, mankind and the divine purpose (or significance) of life. As they explored and chronicled man's history from the Black perspective, I became acutely aware of life's purpose and meaning as it involves the absolute truth of God. Every time I get an opportunity to hear or see another "report" of life on the sands of the Motherland, I find myself able to expand my understanding even further.

Thanks to Mrs. Nancy Sweet (a devoted parishioner of the church which it is my privilege to serve presently), I am a benefactor of her twelve-day visit on the soil of the motherland of humankind. Thanks to her understanding of the significance of life and our responsibility to relate to and chronicle history, I have been able to glean new expanded understandings. Thanks to her diligence in submitting her experience to the form of the written word, the reader-whoever he or she may be, at whatever level of understanding s/he might be-likewise, will benefit.

Once again the torch is being passed on. Indeed another bridge has been built between the past and the present, integrity and insult, right and wrong, God and person. Another opportunity for synthesis of humankind's noblest ideas and deeds has been offered.

Thank you, Sister Sweet, for the opportunity of being a part of your great adventure.

Rev. Pleasant L. Hailey, Jr.
Minister
African Methodist Episcopal Church

Dedication

I dedicate this book to my children
William, Marcus (deceased), Patrick, Sarah, and Lauralynn
As a loving and dedicated Christian mother
I give to them a legacy of commitment and positive perseverance
and a desire to challenge
their own inner strength

Section One

1. A New Beginning
2. The Pyramids and the Sphinx
3. Arrival in Accra, Ghana

A New Beginning

It all started at the Kennedy Airport of New York City on July 26, 1991 with the coming together of over fifty people from many sections of the United States with a single idea in mind:to become a part of the planned "Adventure in Ghana" West Africa trip.

Upon arrival at the airport, my bags were inspected, checked and tagged with a sticker that read, "Accra, Ghana." That in itself was enough to raise my blood pressure a degree or two where it remained for the duration of the trip.

In the airport's upstairs lounge, which was reserved for them, the members slowly arrived. It was amazing that we could sense in each other the excitement and vibes that were bringing us together as one big family. We laughed and joked about our expectations, enjoying ourselves but never losing the seriousness of the impending trip. There were many expressions of the whys and wherefores; however, one single conclusion was evident. We had all decided it was time in our lives to visit the land in which our roots are still firmly planted: in the soil of Mother Africa.

Questions such as: "What is it like over there; will our distant relatives welcome us; how will we feel once we return home?" These and many other thoughts helped to relieve some of the anxiety of the impending plane ride.

Due to a bad rainstorm, many incoming flights to Kennedy Airport were delayed by several hours, therefore the flight to Cairo, Egypt-our first touchdown across the Atlantic-was also delayed several hours. Even this did not dampen our spirits because we were concerned about other group members that might miss the trip. Unconsciously we formed an allegiance with those that were not yet physically a part of the group.

Finally the delayed planes arrived with all of our missing members. Instead of leaving New York at the expected eleven o'clock hour, the take-off time was one a.m. Once underway, it was smooth, uneventful and relaxing. However, between short naps, I experienced a bit of nervousness about being over water for such a long time. My strong faith sustained me and calmed my fears.

Upon our arrival at the airport of Cairo, Egypt, getting through customs and finally arriving at the designated hotel was a welcome relief. However no-one was ready to give up the chance of sightseeing and shopping in the quaint little shops of downtown Cairo. The group got a chance for a warm-up exercise in bargaining and bartering, preparing it for the many opportunities of such to follow.

Up and down the narrow dirt streets, in and out of the small shops we wandered, marveling at the sights and sounds of the city. The shopkeepers were most friendly and welcomed the business we brought.

For many in the group, this was their first time abroad and one could see excitement and anticipation bursting out all over. Musing over the paintings in the art gallery, examining the trinkets of gold, or just browsing in the clothing boutiques kept would-be sleepers awake and involved socially as well as economically in their new surroundings. Finally around three a.m. Sunday morning, rest-broken, sleepy and tired, shut-eye set in and all was well with the world.

The wake-up call, the beginning of a daily ritual, got the group together for a light breakfast before loading on the bus and heading for an adventurous unknown. Hardly any group member realized his or her traditional Sunday morning custom. However, thankfulness was evident in everyone's demeanor.

Seeing downtown Cairo in the daylight gives one a different perspective of the city. Now one could see the conditions under which many of the people live. Scores of the houses are in very poor condition, however, there are large modern buildings with manicured lawns which were sparsely inhabited due to the weekend.

The outskirts or suburban sectors, in contrast to the downtown area, are where one sees the conditions under which most of the Cariene people live. Like the urban area, the housing is inadequate. Vendors line the dirt roads from one end to the other. The elderly and the children are plentiful and many appear to be wandering about aimlessly.

With all the activities going on in and around the city, it's hard to believe it's six a.m., and it's even harder to believe we are on this excursion bus, rolling through the streets of Cairo, Egypt heading for Giza, the sand dune home of the great Pyramids and the mighty Sphinx.

We arrive at this particular site early in the morning with the Universal Sun making its trek over the tip of the largest Pyramid, while the other two stand in a supportive role.

As I gazed upon these mighty examples of the works of a great, colorful, glorious African people, I wondered how the (Eurocentric) American history books could intentionally overlook the builders and contributors to this African society. How can we, African-Americans, continue to forgive and forget the deliberate oversight and misrepresentation of our illustrious ancestors? Will the world ever acknowledge the authentic masters of these complicated edifices?

The children tested their climbing skills while the adults stood in awe of the majestic inhabitants who sent them back in time to a great era of powerful people: their people.

Other sights to behold around the Pyramids were the camels, horses and, of course, the people inhabitants who came daily to meet the tourists and sell their wares. Much picture-taking and some camel back hopping by brave souls proved to be as much fun as it was enlightening. Souvenirs and trinkets were readily available. Across the sand from the Pyramids stood the great Sphinx, who seemingly watched the group as it moved from one small discovery to another. Even though one part of its face is missing from its grand old head, I could not help but marvel at such an imposing figure. What secrets about our people are enshrined within the chiseled-out form that was once simply a large stone? Some of the learned members of the group shared the information about what happened to the lost part of the face of the Sphinx. *Deliberate* cannon shots ordered by Napoleon Bonaparte, one of the many European invaders of Egypt, is responsible for this mutilation.

Leaving the Pyramids, the Sphinx, and saying good-bye to the people who barely eke out a living selling trinkets and camel rides left a sense of sadness within me. However, what a beautiful and exciting way to start an adventure on Motherland soil.

The stay in Cairo was short. The time had come for us to head for the airport and our final destination: Accra, Ghana.

At this juncture, we were all experts in dealing with customs and inpections although we had entered the continent only twenty-four hours ago. (Under certain conditions one learns very fast). Passports, tickets, claim checks, tote bags and even small children were managed with ease. We moved slowly but continously through the lines until at last the exit door loomed before us and everyone gave a sigh of relief. Beyond the exit door was seen the airplane that was waiting to whisk us away to unknown places where we would gain the knowledge which would forever dismiss many of the myths and misconceptions that are a part of our American (Westernized) teachings.

Although the jet plane was not as luxurious as the mighty 747 from New York, we maintained our high level of excitement and anticipation. Two stops were made before finally arriving in Accra, Ghana. Those stops were brief; time did not permit us to leave the plane.

Upon emerging from the plane onto the ramp that led to the descending steps, I paused for a few minutes to look over the barren field, observing the hot sun gently caressing the group of returning descendants. My thoughts turned to several centuries earlier when my ancestors lived and prospered, unhindered, under this same sun. How did things get so mixed up, and what caused the greed of a group of people that would drive them to the point of inhumane acts against another group? Perhaps my brief encounter with my African brothers and sisters, when we walk barefooted in the dust and sand from which I was snatched, yet unborn, will give me a sense of relief when I behold that of which I am part owner.

On through customs we went, and loaded into the waiting bus that made its way to the Sun Lodge Hotel, arriving at approximately five in the afternoon.

The furniture in the hotel restaurant had been used to form a huge round table at which the group sat to receive a briefing and hotel assignments before exposure to the Ghanaian community. Also at this meeting we met the person(s) with whom we would share living quarters for the duration of the trip. This proved to be one of the many highlights of the trip. Each person took on the responsibility of being a brother's/sister's keeper.

By now the hour was late, but hardly anyone was ready to give up or give in to the demands of our tired bodies. Around midnight, lights began to gradually go out and eventually all slept or rested in his/her own way.

Section Two

4. Day One in Accra, Ghana
5. Grandma Alice's Orphanage Home
6. The Reburial of Dr. duBois
7. Kumasi, Home of the Ashante People

As is the custom of Ghana, during our first day, the Chief evoked the blessings of his land upon the group. Also the welcome mat was rolled out symbolically. A brief ceremony consisted of the Chief sipping spirits from his personal cup. Three members of the group-Akbar Muhammad, Nancy Sweet and William Evans-responded to the welcome by receiving the spirits from this same cup. The spirits were hard and real.

Our first full day in Accra was spent taking a tour in and around the city of Accra. We made several stops. They were all interesting, productive, inspirational and informative. The first stop was a meeting with Chief Nii Amugi, the Chief of Greater Accra, the seat of government. He is also the president of the House of Chiefs.

A presentation of a T-shirt, a cap, and a beverage was made to the Chief. These items were symbols of the "Stop the Killing" drive in America in 1990 under the leadership of Minister Louis Farrakhan.

Several probing questions to the Chief were posed from the group. Shirley of Buffalo asked, "What is the length of time of a Chief's rule?" Answer: *It is a lifetime position acquired through inheritance*. Hanifah Muhammad of Memphis asked, "What are the Chief's functions?" *Answer: He is the leader of the people of his particular area, the head of various committees and the president of the Council of Chiefs*. Christopher Muhammad of New York asked, "How is contact made with past ancestors?" *Answer: A designated person is put into a trance where contact is made with spirits. These spirits transmit the information to the person in the trance who passes it on to the Chief, who in turn passes it on to the person seeking spiritual advice*. Virginia X of Boston asked, "Do you have a message for the people in the United States of America?" *Answer: We are all one people now and it is our hope that the Africans in America will come home*. Nancy of Malvern asked, "Under what conditions is the Chief required to step down from office?" *Answer: He is removed from office if found to be corrupt and practices infidelity*. The role of the Chief is still very much a part of the governing apparatus in Ghana.

The second stop was a "working" textile factory in the industrial city of Tema. In reference to factories, the word "working" means that raw material comes into the building and leaves as a finished consumable product.

At this factory we were shown the many intricate ways that raw cotton is machine-printed or hand-blocked by workers into beautiful pieces of material that are sold all over the world. In my limited travels, I am yet to see any pieces of material labeled "made in Tema". The capable guide, Drunnen Heussen, did a fantastic job of walking us through this factory.

There are three stages that cotton must go through in order to become a finished product. The first stage is called preparation for printing and it involves: checking for faults, sewing ends together, passing through buffers to ensure smoothness, fermentation and washing/bleaching. The second stage is called printing. This stage is done either by machines or is hand blocked. The final stage is drying and preparation for dispensing to outlets.

Distributor and more information is available. [1]

Grandma Alice's Orphanage Home

Continuing the trip, the next stop was a visit to the SOS Orphanage Home which is also located in Tema. This Orphanage Home was started by, and remains under the direction of, Alice Appea. Chronologically she is old (mid 80's). However, in mind and spirit, she is young and tuned into the needs and love of her very young to not so young charges.

Listening to the dreams and inspirations that are still high on her agenda for abandoned and homeless children, I could not imagine her leaving her home, even through natural causes.

Grandma Alice, as she is affectionately called, was an only child who longed for playmates. Often the children around her, who were materially less fortunate than she, became welcomed guests in the home of her wealthy parents. From the beginning of her friendship with the children, she wanted them to live with her, to share her belongings and to never leave her home. Often she would convince her parents to provide living quarters for the more destitute of her playmates.

She remains here, in her childhood home. The two seem inseparable. She continues to work and help care for the 182 children in the now multi-building complex. The children seem content, well-nourished and friendly. The home is orderly and well-kept with mannerly children all around, along with small animals that freely roam the beautifully landscaped grounds.

I was most interested in Grandma Alice's recipe for the vitality and longevity of her life. Her comment was, "I have to think about that, but I will let you know." Several days later I received a hand-delivered note written in uneven script. The contents were, "The whole world I feel is my country and to do good is my religion." It was signed, "Grandma Alice."

Several boxes of clothing were left at the Orphanage Home by the group. Also many pledges of financial assistance were given.

Anyone who so desires may support this truly dedicated lady and her humane causes through articles of clothing, money and/or membership in the nationwide association of supporters.[2]

Photographs

THIS PLAQUE IS DEDICATED
TO THE MEMORY OF THE LATE
OSAGYEFO DR. KWAME NKRUMAH
FIRST PRESIDENT OF GHANA AND
FOUNDER OF THE GHANA INSTITUTE OF
JOURNALISM.
UNVEILED BY: MISS JOYCE ARYEE
P.N.D.C. SECRETARY FOR INFORMATION
ON THE OCCASION OF THE SILVER
JUBILEE ANNIVERSARY OF THE
INSTITUTE. 5TH MAY 1984

DIASPORA
P.O. BOX
TEL.

Photos to be read clockwise

Credits

1.AbdulAkbar Muhammad, discussing economic investment opportunities in Ghana

2. First step in African soil: Cairo, Egypt

3.Surveying Kente cloth: so many patterns-which to choose?Inside the market

4. A proud display of the world-renown Kente cloth: inside a Ghanaian sweat-shop

5. Grandma Alice's beloved charges

6. The Mayor of Accra (center), Akbar Muhammad (right), the assistant to the Mayor (left)

7. Entrance of the Ghana Institute of Journalism, founded by first president Dr. Kwame Nkrumah

8. Seaside town, on route to the woodcarving center of Aburi

9. Home of Abdul Akbar Muhammad: "Brother Akbar"

10. Haunted doorways, grim reminders: the entrance of the Cape Coast "castles"

11. Wall of the inner dungeon, Cape Coast

12. The courtyard of the "castle", where African women were "displayed" and disrespected by the male European traders

13. Where world civilization was refined: the pyramids at Giza, Egypt

14. African mothers welcome African children: may the circle be unbroken

The Reburial of Dr. DuBois

The DuBois Centre in Accra, Ghana is a place to be held in awe. Here one meets through wall hangings (framed pictures) many of the pioneers and forerunners who paved the way and smoothed the rocky road for others who are now coming in increasing numbers. They are seeking a way through the dark paths of rejection, annihilation, and racism that continue to confront and confound Black people all over the world.

The video presentation of the reburial of Dr. DuBois, at his tomb, in his own yard, was heart-rendering. Many dignitaries attended the dedication ceremony. Among them were Maya Angelou, the Ambassador of China, DuBois' son, and others including Dr. Mohammad Ben-Abdallah, Minister of Culture for the PNDC-the official government in Accra.[3] After viewing the video, Dr. Ben-Abdallah delivered the first of several informative and educational lectures that the group would hear during the twelve day trip.

Dr. Ben-Abdallah's stirring message to the group appeared to have touched the nerve of each individual present. It was a "wake-up call" that aroused within all a sense of belonging: a challenge to go into your archives, learn the history of your people, feel the flame that continues to burn, and light the way for others following in your footsteps, which should be so large and definable that none can miss the direction in which you are going.

Dr. Ben-Abdallah reflected a vision, painted a mental picture, to show how his government is working to realize the dream of Dr. DuBois. To paraphrase, he said to build bridges between Africa and America. Bring together the best that each has to offer. Make sure that you create within the children an awareness of the contributions to society made by great Black leaders. Everyone must get involved, because the African struggle is Black America's struggle also.

After his lecture, we gave Dr. Ben-Abdallah an extended standing ovation with many cheers, tears and accolades, followed by questions and comments. Following is a sampling of the varied, thought-provoking and timely questions from the group.

Joanna X from New York asked, "Did Nkrumah ever come back to Ghana?" *Answer: No, the people didn't welcome him back, however, his body was returned to Ghana.* [4] Minister Charles Muhammad asked, "What leaders of today do you see carrying on or who will carry on the spirit and dream of great people?" *Answer: Events unfolding today that demand great leaders are certain to provide the leadership necessary to carry on in the DuBois tradition.* Stephen X of Chicago asked, "Can we see a parallel between DuBois /Garvey and Rawlings/Nkrumah?" *Answer: It is possible. Here we see [two] seemingly opposing individuals coming at each other on a direct collision course. However, if we examine closely their ideas and ideals, we will see solid, straightforward human beings who desperately wanted or still want to "right the wrong" done to their people.*

Khalifah of Newport News, Virginia, asked, "Many of us have heard many of the legendary things about Chairman Rawlings. Would you tell us a little about him?" *Answer: This will not be very impartial since I am a part of Rawlings' government. But he is a hands-on kind of leader. For example, when he goes out into the countryside, or other places, and sees the need for a sewage system, or a well for water, he immediately orders the appropriate people to fix the problem. He is not an ideologist. He cuts through the red tape and deals directly with the problem.*

I am convinced that each individual will carry forever in his or her heart the soul-searching, yet rewarding, words of a truly great warrior who seems to be the embodiment of all those Black leaders that we must hold up for generations to come, lest we forget from whence we came.

Six o'clock in the morning seems to be the magic time for getting on the road, or perhaps that is the time of least resistance. What body is awake and of sound mind at such an hour? Nevertheless, everyone seems to manage the necessities of life, gathering up whatever is needed, including babies and small children. They make their way onto the waiting excursion bus, occupy a seat, allowing a comatose-like state to take over for awhile. Our destination for this particular morning was Kumasi, home of the once-powerful rulers of Ghana, known as the Ashante people [the Ashantehene]. Once in Kumasi, the first place to visit is the historic military museum which was used as a fort to house the military as well as to protect the city.

For many years the countries of Africa that were colonized by the British were forced to fight against each other under British rule. With the gaining of freedom in some countries, the Africans united against the British. In this museum, one finds artifacts and remnants of war that either were won, donated or confiscated by Africans who fought for the British against Italy, Germany and other enemies. Of course, other items on the fort tell part of the story of the Ghanaian's eventual fight against these same Britons for their own independence. The Ashante people are hoping to receive contributions that will enable them to restore and maintain this museum.

The next site to visit is the King's Court where he sits on certain days to handle concerns of his people. All legal matters are handled by the King and his sub-kings. Kingship is hereditary and is a lifetime position. Unlike in the days of old, the present-day King has only one wife who has her own living quarters. The group seemed interested in the fact that the Queen is not the King's wife, but usually his mother or sister.

After leaving the King's Court, we go directly to the King's Palace, located on a large site surrounded by unusual and interesting shrubbery, plants and exotic flowers of all kinds. Grounds keepers and guards met us at the gates and escorted the group to the large front steps where we were told that, due to a heavy weekend schedule of varied activities, the King was resting and was unable to greet visitors at this hour. However, he relayed greetings through staff members and wished the group well. Some of us were disappointed about his decision not to see us because we had high hopes of seeing a "real palace" occupied by a "bona fide King" in all his glory.

We survived the disappointment and recuperated in good time because next on out itinerary is lunch time. We dine at Rose's Guest House restaurant. The atmosphere was warm and pleasant and the food was nourishing as well as appetizing.

On to the group's next stop: Ghana's Natural Centre where dancers performed beautiful pieces such as, "The Executioners", "The Royal Dance", "The War Dance, the fast one", and "The Fetish Dance". The dancers were lively and highly appreciated by the group. The dance company is available for outside performances if sponsors become available. Contact may be made through Ghana's Cultural Center, located in Kumasi, Ghana.

Excitement and jubilation abound among the group members because the next stop of visitation is the village where the beautiful and colorful Kente Cloth is woven. It is plentiful and relatively inexpensive. Purchasing lists were long as great expectations permeated the minds of all. Plans for purchasing the cloth for gifts as well as for personal use were high on our agenda. I was excited about finally having the chance to purchase a tablecloth for my dining-room table. Not even getting lost on the bumpy-lumpy, narrow winding road dampened our spirits.

Finally the big bus arrives in the seemingly quiet village. However, within a matter of seconds (it seemed) it was totally surrounded by villagers-mostly young children-offering pieces of material to the group.

Some of the group members got off the bus and attempted to bargain with the potential sellers. This proved to be disastrous because the villagers out-numbered the unprepared group members, who hurriedly returned to the bus for safety.

A suggestion was made that we go to the Chief's quarters and check out his selections of material before making purchases. We made our way slowly, up the winding stairway to a small room reserved for the Chief. The sun had set, therefore the only light available to us came from the heavens. The door was to have been locked from the inside while inspection of material was made. There were many designs and patterns, each having a special name and meaning.

Unfortunately, the entrance door was not closed in time to prevent an influx of villagers and group members to fill the large room to capacity and more. Because of the congestion, it soon became apparent that it was dangerous to conduct bargaining here. The room was emptied of all people.

Downstairs in the courtyard and in the parking area pandemonium accelerated to a degree that all of us, including the villagers, were in danger of being seriously hurt. Fortunately, the peaceful spirit of the African villagers prevented a state of panic from occurring.

In a corner of the parking area away from the turmoil, some of the village children and I were engaged in a friendly conversation. Their understanding of English was slight, however, we were able to communicate out thoughts to each other. They were all interested in coming to America because they had heard that books, shoes and pretty clothes were plentiful. I told them that their clothes were very lovely and that we were in the village to get material to take back to America so the Americans could see what *their* clothes were like. That pleased them. They were also jubilant over the two pencils and extra pieces of writing paper that I shared with them.

I was surrounded by dozens of excited children and completely cut off from the bus. Realizing that this was a somewhat precarious position to be in, I started moving in the direction of the bus. Then children started moving towards me making it impossible to move. At this point I could feel a tinge of panic settling in. Fortunately, a fallen tree was close by and, needless to say, I climbed on it yelling to the group members. They were unable to hear my voice because the children were also yelling. They thought that I was having fun. In fear and frustration I stopped yelling and miraculously so did they. I made my way to the bus where eventually all group members, some a bit shaken from the experience, settled in their seats, regained their composure and evaluated their experience. Some members examined their purchases while those who were unable to get the much-desired material reflected, with regret, on how the great possibility of making large purchases did not materialize because of our misunderstanding of how impromptu business deals are handled in some of the market -places.

With all group members aboard, the big bus slowly pulled away from the village, retracing its tracks on the winding road that would eventually take us back to the hotels.

Even though our visit to the Royal Kente Cloth market did not meet our expectations, we were thrilled by having the opportunity of experiencing the exuberance of our distant relatives. As with other mass gatherings, we, the African-Americans, felt the kinship and the warm hospitable overtures from our brothers and sisters of the Motherland.

Section Three

8. Downtown Accra: The Investment Centre
9. The City Hall of Accra
10. The Ghana Institute of Journalism
11. The Art Center
12. The Residence of the Mayor of Accra

At the Investment Centre, Mr. Korsa-Dick, the director of administration, welcomed us on behalf of the mayor, "who is attending to other official business". We are at downtown Accra where we will visit the Business Investment Centre of Accra and the office of the Regional Secretary [Mayor], meet the director of the Ghana Institute of Journalism (GIJ), shop at the Art Centre, visit the Mayor's residence, and end the day by viewing a film entitled "Heritage".

The Investment Centre is set up by the government so that all business matters can be transacted in one central place. The main purpose of the center is to interpret investment law. The key role is: to promote investment, identify and formulate projects, and hold seminars and conferences relative to business and investment purposes.

According to the director there are several areas that interest the Ghanaian people, such as agriculture. According to Korsa-Dick: *The land is here; we have it and also the resources. We are capable of using your financial support so that we can jointly develop your ideas. Some facets of agriculture that hold our attention are: planting, harvesting, and marketing.*

Other interesting ideas are Housing Development and Tourism. The two areas are interdependent. In order to have viable tourism, we must possess affordable and accessible housing, not only for the tourist but for our own people as well. It would be very difficult to attract outsiders to our cities if our own people are lacking in the fundamental necessities of a healthy and productive lifestyle.

Those who may be interested in the above areas for investment purposes should consult section 21 of the Government Approval Board [Investment rules and Regulations] which, in essence, states that anyone wishing to invest in Ghana must bring in foreign capital. The minimum amount for investment purposes is sixty thousand dollars and a hundred thousand dollars for ownership.

An investor would have his or her own personnel so as not to displace the existing Ghanaian work force. Some of the benefits from investments are that shareholders could easily acquire passports. All supporting staff would come under the quota system. Another feature of this system is that it would allow one to readily transfer money to Ghanaian banks. Also, the protection of the law of foreign investors protects the investor by forcing all applicants to go through the Government

Approval Board, where there is access to world markets with a guarantee of OPEC [Organization of Petroleum Exporting Countries] protection. Interested future applicants may contact: Mr. Korsa-Dick, Director of Administration, Box 385, A.M.A., Accra, GHANA.

The tourist director gave a brief overview of his department. To paraphrase, according to him: *The tourist business is a young one that the government recently started promoting. The main purpose of this department is to promote cultural and historical knowledge of our society. Our major interests are: awareness, especially of events before the advent of Europeans to our country, exhibiting methods of farming that have a concentration on herbal mixing for medicinal purposes, and Black contact as well as other groups.*

Several group members addressed the director with comments or questions. Dr. Ali from Sacramento asked, "If starting a Youth Cultural Exchange program, may we have a letter of support from you (the director) that would allow our youth to participate in your culture and vice-versa?" *Answer: That information is available.*[5] Answers to other questions can be found in the director's overview.

Our second stop of the day is City Hall. The Mayor was away on official business. Mr. Korrsse, director of administration, presided in his behalf. The Mayor's officers were presented, followed by self-introductions of each group member, and a formal welcome by the director.

A presentation of Accra by director Korrsse included several key points of interest such as Accra is the seat of government with a population upward of 2 million. The two house council was established in 1898 and it became a city in 1961.

The city's responsibilities are: sanitation, slaughter houses, to build and furnish educational institutions; to promote programs for the welfare of the people; to provide children's centers; to promote tourism and care for the gardens.

A response to the director's welcome was made by Brother Akbar Muhammad. His comments, in brief, were: *It is not the little things you have to offer, but the greatness and vastness you have. There are those from America who want to assist you. For example, two ambulances are waiting in Chicago for Accra, gifts from that great city. There are also other items available to you.* Mr. Korrsse commented, "We are unable to get the donated items because of lack of contact with Chicago." Mr. Korrsse was told whom to contact in Chicago in order to get the ambulances shipped immediately.

In addition to Brother Akbar's comments, there were other statements and questions from the group. Nora from Philadelphia asked, "Is there anyone here to speak on behalf of health issues; how are you handling this problem?" *Answer: Yes. We are concerned with health problems. We have a Department of Health, with a medical staff who is concerned with environmental conditions and cleanliness. The clinics are also maintained by them. Overall health care is under the Ministry of Health.* Ralph of St. Louis asked, "How is the city structured; how does it work?" *Answer: The apex is the assembly which is made up of two-third elected officials and one-third appointed officials by the government, taking into consideration their background and contributions. The two-third members group meets monthly.* The director omitted the duties of the one-third group.

Additional comments by the director further clarified the working of the officials. To summarize his comments: There are committees in the assembly to meet certain needs. Each sub-committee level is responsible for six areas in order to decentralize the power so that towns may govern their own citizens. The chairperson of each sub-committee reports to the assembly.

Stephen X of Chicago asked, "What particular imagery is coming out the United States to Ghana, and how do Ghana's youth view the United States?" *Answer: Too long have the two groups been kept apart. There should be opportunities for them to come together. We are working on plans to develop this part of the world. We need to develop our resources and explore our communalities. Such areas as music and clothes are areas that each country's youth understands*. Leigh from New York asked, "How do you see Ghana in reference to political and social bases?" *Answer: We are aware of the collapse of your banks. This affects us as well. However, we are doing well so far. We are confident that no-one can take us for a ride. We are in a good position to maintain what we have and the future is promising. We will need the cooperation of honest investors, who will come, not with evil motives, but with genuine investment purposes. The future is bright, and we welcome more expertise.*

Khalifah from Virginia asked, "One of the big problems we have in the Black community in America is what we call the brain drain. Our Black professionals take badly needed skills and services out of their own community for opportunities elsewhere. What is Ghana doing to keep its professionals in Ghana? And what is Ghana doing to ensure that when students leave Ghana to become professionals, they will complete their studies and come home?" The question was not answered fully. In short, the director stated: We don't want to do anything to keep our people from going abroad for educational opportunities.

Once again, Brother Akbar commented. To summarize his statement: *We would like to be included in your trade shows. You are our marketing target for the next five years. The plan is in the works and as soon as we have finalized that plan and the materials arrive, we will move forward.* There were other questions and comments from the group. Charles Muhammad from Toledo commented. "We had a hundred youth ready to come, but the details were too late. However we are planning to come at a later time." Nora from Philadelphia asked, "How can you make it easier for the investors to get started?" *Answer: One should follow these steps: 1) register your request with the Investment Centre, 2) get it approved by the government approval board, 3) you should have in place the capabilities of operating your own business independently of us, although we will gladly give you the necessary support for your success, and 4) send the completed application to us. It is very important that you check closely all details and respond accordingly.*

Again, Charles Muhammad from Toledo asked, "How does one get an introductory letter?" *Answer: First decide exactly what you want and then put it in writing and send it to the Investment Centre, attention of Korsa-Dick.* Stephen X of Chicago asked, "What exactly do you want from us in reference to running our own investment firm?" *Answer: Nothing. You can come here, follow the steps outlined above, and run your own business. We are very positive towards you. You are welcome to come here and set up your own business.*

The meeting was closed with final comments in brief from Brother Akbar, sponsor of the "Adventure in Ghana": "Today's greatest opportunity is occurring abroad. One-third of the world is undeveloped economically by the West; the door of opportunity is open. We are trained by good western schools, therefore our skills are available, in place, and the chance to construct economic foundations is in Africa. Guarantees in life do not exist. Seize the opportunity and risk success. Come to Africa with your expertise-the Motherland welcomes you."

In reference to a comment concerning Ghanaian citizenship: the potential citizen must a) be born in Ghana or b) give up present citizenship through the Ghanaian naturalization process. There is movement toward dual citizenship for African-Americans vis-á-vis Ghana.

Final comments from the director were, "Thanks to all of you from all of us."

With minds reeling with the prospects of new adventures and investment in Ghana, we met with Mr. Kojo Yankah, director of the G.I.J., the Ghana Institute of Journalism. He started his talk with a short and informative history of Ghana's struggle for independence in 1957.

To summarize: *Many men, mostly young, fought, or went to prison while others gave the last measure of their lives for the freedom that finally came. After the war for independence, the leader of the struggle had many priorities. One such priority was to establish a journalism school so that information could be truthfully disseminated throughout Ghana as well as other places in the world. The specific purpose of the Institute was, and still is, to spread the ideas of freedom in an unbiased way. Africans from other countries are brought here and trained as journalists and then are returned to their own countries with the necessary skills. The [original] vision continues to capture the potential journalists who come here from many parts of the world.*

Prospective: A two year diploma course with the last half of the second year spent in the field getting practical and hands-on training. General courses are: social science, political science, psychology, shorthand and various other courses relative to becoming a journalist. There are specialized courses for those who want the skills for a specific aspect of writing. During their field experience the opportunity arises for the students to learn what real "in the trenches" journalism is all about. The school is very successful and we are confident that it is impacting upon world opinion today.

Mr. Yankah gave a chronology of the regimes of Ghana between 1957-1982, the last of which continues today. He ended his talk about the G.I.J. with the following remarks: "Our Institute is different from many other institutes in that in continues the liberation movement for which it was founded."

In addition to holding the directorship of the G.IJ., he is a renown author. He recently released a book entitled **Namibia**, which is an in-depth study of the people of Namibia's struggle for freedom. He is also the author of a book on Ghana's current [1991] Head of State, Chairman John J. Rawlings: **The Trials of J.J. Rawlings**, which was not available.

A brief synopsis of the events leading up to Namibia's freedom ended the presentation. It was followed by current facts on Namibia, and comments and questions from the group.

Facts about Namibia

- Whites occupy 90% of the land mass of the country.

- Presently [1991], UN Resolution 432, which is concerned with the 90% of land that the whites now own, is in debate.

- Native people of Namibia know little about their homeland.

- Neighbors are separated from neighbors, having been told that the other is unfriendly, hostile, and did not want to associate or mingle with anyone else.

- Whites came and methodically killed, or pushed off, the owners of the land until only 10% of the land was occupied by the original people.

At this juncture I would like to pose this question to the aboriginal people of the Americas: does this tactic seem familiar?

Some of the questions directed to Mr. Yankah were very thought-provoking. Mary Dennis of Chicago asked, "Do other tribes [sic] now know what happened to the people of Namibia?" *Answer: They are now being given the truth about how and why they have such a small portion of their land.* Khalifah from Virginia commented, "Those who think that the idea of moving the South Africans from their land is a unique idea should search the history books of America where there exist numerous accounts of how the Europeans used the same process in the American Indians' plight. Also, Mr. Yankah, please tell us about the incredible mineral wealth in Namibia." Response from Mr. Yankah: "The brother is on target concerning the Namibian people's removal from their land, which is very rich in minerals and other natural resources." Stephen X from Chicago asked, "How were you able to get your book out of Namibia?" *Answer: It went mainly through the ministers who had some freedom of movement.*

At this point, Mr. Yankah spoke of how successful the journalists are in getting the information out of the country of Namibia to outsiders. Hopefully others will read about their conditions and get involved in this cause. The Ghana Institute of Journalism feels confident that the eruptions taking place today are mainly the results of the Institute's journalists out in the field spreading the information and work about the liberation movement.

Another concern from the group was that of the fate of the Whites in Namibia. This is one of the major problems facing the new government-what to do about the White farmers who occupy huge acres of land. Their holdings consist of the best of the land in the country. Some of the White farmers have said that, in essence, if their farms (which they took from the people of Namibia) are divided among the indegenous people, they would leave the area. Some are leaving already.

Isn't it ironic that the white farmers feel that they are the ones against whom injustice is directed? What short memories they have.

Mr. Yankah made his book **Namibia** available to the group at the end of the session.

The Art Center

The presentation and subsequent information concerning the work of the Ghana Institute of Journalism and the following discussion of the turmoil in Namibia was temporarily stored in the corner of our brain so we could, once again, indulge in shopper's delight.

Upon approaching the multi-building complex I was baffled by why it was called the Art Center. However, once through the main entrance, my question and bafflement immediately vanished while my senses simultaneously responded to this never-before-felt experience.

First of all my eyes saw bold bright colors that were beyond description. Think of a color, any color, and it was there. Imagine designs and patterns so intricate, innovative, and compelling that they would cause one to stare in awe at what the Ghanaian people are able to do with colors.

While my eyes were gawking, my hands reached out and touched some of the nearby garments. Some were smooth while others were crinkled, furry, stiff, and even prickly. Each texture was appropriately used to express an opinion or make a fashion statement. In addition to the garments, there were trinkets of all sorts, statues of every description, jewelry that would blow anyone's mind, household items, furniture, and other paraphernalia.

Also, my nose was hard at work, experiencing new smells. In several areas of the center were native dishes of fruits, nuts, breads, stews, and other palatable dishes that enticed the mouth to exercise its purpose. Unfortunately, or maybe fortunately, I was unable to sample everything. Nevertheless, I left the center with a well-defined idea of what African foods are all about.

Being involved in such a display of human activities, one might conclude that the ears were not involved in the happenings. That is a false assumption. On the contrary, my ears, abiding by their traditional role, perked up at the unusual and unique sounds that they were unfamiliar with. Musical instruments of all shapes and sizes provided some of these sounds. Although most of the Ghanaian's language was beyond our understanding, we managed to make purchases and enjoy the fellowship of our people. Children yelling and running about gleefully were a joy to see.

The main purpose of the Art Center is for economic reasons. Hundreds of vendors from all over the country come daily to sell their goods. For many of the people here, this is their main source of income.

Most of the members in the group were elated to bargain with the vendors. This is a fun as well as a productive activity, because one must be able to wrangle with the sellers but at the same time use sound judgment in order to strike a fair price for everyone. We spent several hours over a period of days browsing, bartering, and enjoying the atmosphere of the center. It is easy to spend hours at a time there without experiencing a minute of boredom. The Ghanaians are knowledgeable about their merchandise and enjoy the opportunity to display their skills. Although there is a language barrier, most of us managed, through signs and body language, to communicate. There were also guides available if the need arose.

At the conclusion of our first in-depth Art Center experience, we returned to the bus and headed for the Mayor's residence in order to get first-hand information about his city.

The grounds were formal and the Mayor most cordial. His introductory remarks, which included a warm, friendly welcome, were short. This was followed by a brief history of the country and a fervent plea for all of us Africans, on both sides of the Atlantic Ocean, to work together in order to move Africa along to complete freedom from the exploitation and misuse by those who do not have the best interest of Africa at heart.

The Mayor accepted questions from the group. Cherry of New York asked, "How do you, the Chiefs, and the Elders work together?" *Answer: Before my time, there was ceremonial rule. Now my staff, which includes Elders and Chiefs, work together as a unit*. Hanifah from Memphis asked, "What is the number one problem facing you?" *Answer: Discipline is the greatest problem. It is very difficult to get the people to listen and do what is necessary to solve our problems, especially the sanitation one*. Joanna from New York asked, "What mayoral change is needed within the next five years?" *Answer: The ability of the people to meet their tax obligation is the one most pressing at this time*. Khalifah from Virginia asked, "What was your job before becoming Mayor of Ghana?" *Answer: I was an accountant at the University of Ghana*.

Someone from the group raised the question of welfare and means by which some segments, especially the elderly, are cared for. The Mayor's comment was, "We have no welfare system here. All segments of our population, including the elderly and infirm, remain in the home where they are cared for by family members. Neglect of the elderly and infirm is considered to be inhumane and intolerable under our rule."

Several members from the group made presentations to the Mayor. They were given as tokens of friendship and appreciation for the hospitality shown by the Mayor and his immediate household. Cool beverages were served throughout our visit.

The day after the meeting with the Mayor, we were told that he was, in fact, no longer the Mayor, even while he was receiving us. He had been relieved of his position two days before. This was interesting, but did not in any way detract from the gracious hospitality he showed the group.

The final activity of this particular day was the viewing of the film *Heritage* which brought back unpleasant memories and stirred deep emotions among some film members. Much discussion took place after the conclusion of the film. On the bus and into the late hours of the night, some members wrestled with the contents and message of the film that we, here in America, **still** find hard to deal with.

Section Four

13. The Castles of Cape Coast
14. Time Out
15. The Village of Aburi

Never again...Always remembered...

The Castles of Cape Coast

Looking from the Sun Lodge Restaurant, I can see the big excursion bus waiting at the end of the long driveway for its passengers. Everyone hurries along with small children, video equipment, and other paraphernalia that makes for wide-eyed and enthusiastic tourists. All aboard and ready to roll.

The driver, realizing our destination is in the opposite direction from the one in which the bus is headed, backs into a nearby driveway. Ordinarily, this would have solved the problem, but the driveway, like most driveways in this section of town, are unpaved and soft, causing the loaded bus to sink to its axles.

The experienced driver tried all his tricks and maneuvering skills to get the bus going, but to no avail. Within a few minutes, an astute passenger summed up the situation and brilliantly came to the conclusion that "We are stuck." At last we were given the chance to put the democratic process, agreed upon by all members, into action. Early on, Brother Akbar had stressed this process and how it must be used throughout the trip. Consequently, after a brief discussion involving the many experts, it was decided that if everyone would get off the bus, it could then be pushed from its earthy entrenchment by the brothers: a very wise decision. After several rockings back and forth, the bus moved forward.

Standing on the sidelines, saddened by my inability to help, I could not resist taking pictures of the heroics of the strong brothers. There was a job to be done, and they rose to the occasion. Even in their strain, some were smiling. Finally the problem is solved, everyone returns to the bus and we are on the road heading for the Slave Castles and the West African Historical Museum in the city of Cape Coast.

These castles were built originally for military purposes, but were soon converted into holding stations for the Africans stolen from their villages. They were sent to America where they were sold like inanimate objects to be used to build a thriving economy that became the foundation upon which it-America- stands today. Some of the wealth-seeking European-Americans justified the sale of these helpless human beings by calling it a necessary work force for the betterment and prosperity of the country. Some argued also that the captives would fare better in a so-called "civilized" nation. I differ with that argument. How can any system designed to dehumanize someone to a state of worthlessness in his/her own eyesight be of benefit to that individual?

The Liberian refugee campsite was seen along the road to Cape Coast. There appeared to be few facilities for the great number of people brought there because of the uninhabitable conditions in their own country [1991], which, I was informed, was going through a terrible upheaval, in the form of a four-sided civil war.

Unlike the other day trips, this one seemed to have an atmosphere of nervous energy. Perhaps it was because of an anticipatory feeling of what was to come. Our senses were heightened by bits and pieces of information gleamed from other meetings and lectures. Finally, we would be able to have a personal encounter there, where the realities of American slavery had its beginning, and to walk in the same soil where our ancestors spent their last months, as a free people, in their beloved homeland. Here we could touch the buildings that housed them against their will; stare at the big guns, pointed in all directions, to prevent any notion of escape. Most painful of all, we would hear, from the African guides, the horrific ordeals that no living creature should have to endure. Once again, we listened; we endured.

Because of limited time, we were able to visit only two of the many castles in the area. However, from conversations, questions, and responses, it seems that each castle is similar to the others. They were used, in reference to that slave trade, primarily as holding stations for the would-be slaves.

The Historical Museum is an interesting place. Here are found artifacts of African culture from many parts of the continent. There are tools of the fishing trade, hunting paraphernalia, baskets of all sorts, weapons, and other items that were unfamiliar and without identification, although many of the items were labeled with its use and a short history.

Let it be known and understood that the captured Africans were free, peace-loving people who, for hundreds of years, had thrived and prospered under their own rule. Through cruelty, trickery, and any other means at their disposal, the British, the Portugese, and other European nations, succeeded in filling the cargo ships with unsuspecting captured Africans. They were transported to other parts of the world dominated by European people. There, they were sold to the highest bidder. The tour guides emphatically reiterated the horrible conditions and circumstances that prevented many of the captives from surviving the "middle passage".

The first castle on our agenda is St. George. It was built by the Portuguese and later taken by force from them by the British who used it for housing their seat of government. Subsequently, once the idea of the lucrative demand for manpower by the Americans across the Atlantic Ocean surfaced, they used these buildings to store their "cargo", meaning the Africans. The second castle visited by the group was El Mino, similar in build and purpose.

Upon reaching the castle grounds, we were joined by a tour guide who escorted us around and through St. George's castle. He started the commentary with a brief history of the builders and how the physical buildings had gone back and forth from one country's ownership to another. However, it was not until the gold trade began to wane that the then-British owners started seeking other means of revenue. Unfortunately for the Africans, news reached the British headquarters that across the Atlantic Ocean there was a need for workers to till the soil that had the potential of producing this new commodity-cotton. Thus we had the beginning of a system that would go to any length to fill its coffers. Consequently, the Europeans-British, French, Belgian, Spanish, Portugese, and Dutch- and the European-Americans teamed up to present to the world a most hideous act that one group of people imposed upon another group.

Once through the introductory history of the castle, we were walked across the courtyard which was routinely used to display several female captives. Officers from the British military could look down, from their position atop the building, and select the one(s) that would be brought to their quarters for their pleasure. If the woman became pregnant as a result of the officer's lust, they were sent back to a village-not necessarily the one where they previously lived-to bear forever the burden of humiliation, degradation and violent misuse of our beautiful sisters.

The large courtyard was surrounded by several doors and outlets. One door with a sign over it read "Confinement room". This room was originally used to hold rebellious pirates who tried to steal the treasures from ships at sea. Here in this small room, void of all necessities, even food and water, they were left to die. Needless to say, the European opportunist soon began to use this method of punishment for anyone who in any small way thought about bending a rule, much less breaking it. Often the wrong person was confined, but that made no difference. The fate of the confined never changed. Right, wrong or indifferent, once a person passed through this confinement door, death was the only recourse.

Over the top of the confinement door is a symbol. This symbol is in the shape of a star, which looks like the Star of David, widely used by a renown religious sect. In this case, it is a calling card that reveals to the world the contributions, by that religious group, to the capturing and processing of the stolen Africans; their shame is indelible, therefore it cannot be eradicated or disputed.

Two other doors also have very prominent signs. One sign reads "male dungeon", while the other reads "female dungeon". I was at the end of the line that was going through the "female dungeon" door. Facing this small door, tears began to roll down my cheeks, and my body trembled with the chilling revelation that my grandmothers, be they great, great-great, or more, had passed, earlier on, through that door.

Overcome by grief and a momentary desire for retaliation, I turned and walked to the nearby steps where I remained seated for awhile in order to regain my composure before rejoining the group who was silently observing the physical structure of the room. It was approximately the size of a regular bedroom with a small opening near the ceiling. This opening served as both light and ventilation. Needless to say, when the sun went down, the room was dark. The original floor, according to the guide, was dirt. However, as the captives relieved themselves, and as death claimed many of them, the composition of the floor changed.

We were walking on the remains of our ancestors. The human scent, after more than three hundred years, is very much a part of that dungeon. The space could possibly accommodate a total of thirty people; however, it was said that hundreds of captives at the same time were held for months until they would pass through the small "door of no return" onto the waiting ships that would take them across the Atlantic Ocean to America. They would end up on auction blocks and into the hands of merciless financiers, known in history as "slave owners".

Food and water were scarce. The small amounts that were available were brought to the door and thrown up for grabs. Many died trying to get a morsel to eat. In addition to starvation and being trampled to death, disease was another great killer. Even the pregnant women and the children born in captivity were denied any sort of consideration or care. Nevertheless we survived, and the determination passed down from generation to generation by our ancestors urges us to try and prick the conscience of those responsible for the atrocities, the injustice, the second-class citizenship, and the other forms of oppression that African-Americans experience today. None in America, African or non-African, will find peace until compensatory measures and reparations bring the African-American sector on par with all other ethnic groups, especially those of European extraction.

The wide opening at the end of the tunnel where the "door of no return" led was the gateway through which a man and a woman coming from his/her respective dungeon met before walking the gangplank to the small boat that led them to the waiting cargo ship. They were loaded like cattle without any consideration for their safety. Men and women alike were chained, and put in dingy and unsanitary compartments on the ships. Control was not a problem because most of the captives, after months of confinement and starvation, were unable physically, as well as mentally, to overcome the horrible treatment and conditions awaiting them. As before in the dungeons, many did not survive. The bottom of the Atlantic Ocean is littered with the remains of the ships' human cargo that received a watery grave.

After the dungeons we went to other rooms in the castle. One of interest was the Worship Room. Here the captors came and upon bent knees prayed for the continuation of their good fortune: the capture and selling of the Africans. In this same room at different times came the captives who prayed that their bondage would come to an end.

At one point the captives' bondage in the dungeons did end, yet dungeon removal ensured the captives that the worse was yet to come. Across the great Atlantic the guarantees waited.

⌘⌘⌘⌘

It has been said that the spirit never dies. After their castle experience, many members spoke of the eerie feeling of returning to a place of which we had never been a part, yet we could sense the presence of others besides the group members. Listening to different conversations, my mind drifted back to my childhood, years ago when I would try to coax my grandmother to tell me about her mother. Now I have a better understanding of why my grandmother never talked about her past. Perhaps what she had witnessed and heard was too painful to discuss, and this was her way of sparing her family the mental suffering that she knew would come with knowledge of the inhuman treatment of our people. Another train of thought foremost in our minds was forgiveness. Everyone left teary-eyed, wondering how any of the African captives survived not only the brutalizing treatment of the dungeons, and the humiliating female displays in the courtyard, but also the long, diseased journey across the ocean.

Many were searching self to affirm their commitments to do even more to bring about the liberation of all African people, here and abroad. It will be hard for any African, whether in Africa or in America, to remove from our minds the horrors imposed intentionally by Europeans after the "dungeon experience".

The second castle visited by the group, El Mino, was similar in structure and purpose. An informal survey of the group members brought out the fact that others had experienced feelings of deep anguish and momentary hatred, as I had. Guides on the tour told us that it was a common occurrance among African groups touring the castles to experience these feelings.[6]

Happy day. The eighth day in Ghana was set aside for everyone to have a chance to sleep in, to leisurely enjoy the quietness and to reflect on the many activities of the past seven days, or to continue in the fast lane for some. What will the group members do? I will take a sampling later on to find out how different members used their free time.

I choose this time, for the most part of the day, to stay in my room. The quiet voices and activities of the hotel attendants enable me to organize my notes and allow my mind and body to relax for a few hours.

Between 12:00 noon and four p.m, there were two special sessions held: The Ju'maah prayer and a special reception.

Ju'maah prayer during the Adventure in Ghana

The following is an account of the Ju'maah prayer,
as witnessed by Ibn H. Khalif Khalifah,
one of several young men on the trip.

In the capital of Accra the believing (Muslim) men of the trip marched off to Ju'maah Friday prayer services as the rest of the party continued their last minute frenzied shopping

.After a medium distance walk we arrived at a walled-off enclosure shaded by a number of trees. It was literally standing, or in this case, kneeling room only. As we entered, we observed the women and children to the side of the worshippers. The women filled the air with the pungent scents of their foods and other wares (for sale) as the rest of the people [including women] were listening the Imam (Islamic minister) gave the [khutba] (sermon).

Just as we were forewarned, all of the men were in the front while the women who were participating in the services were in the back. For this reason, and this reason only, Brother Akbar Muhammad warned the sisters on the trip not to attend Ju'maah unless they still wished to. (Men and women are separated in the Nation of Islam services, but they are seated to the opposite sides of each other [7] and not the women to the back of the men, clearly an insulting position for the woman.) I would estimate there was anywhere from 500-1000 worshippers in attendance. I wondered to myself, as we worshipped Allah (God) how the people prayed when the weather turned less than favorable. I hadn't noticed any nearby indoor mosque (Islamic worship building).

The population of Ghana, according to different individuals we questioned, is anywhere between 40-70% Muslim. As always, praying with a group is a more powerful experience than doing so alone. This time was no different and I was glad I had attended.

⌘⌘⌘⌘⌘

It is late afternoon and some members are returning to the hotel with evidence of an enjoyable day. Nora of Philadelphia had spent ten hours and used eight packs of hair getting her own hair braided. Several members returned to the Art Center for more browsing and buying, while others visited the Post Office to send off cards and letters to relatives and friends.

H. Khalif Khalifah was picked up at the hotel, spent the afternoon, and had dinner with a husband and wife team of journalists, Bill and MaryEllen Ray, who have lived in Ghana for more than 20 years. They have been regular correspondents to one of his newspapers, *The National NewportNews & Commentator*. Later, Mr. Ray took Khalifah for a ride into the countryside and on to the seacoast opposite the one visited earlier by the group. He did not realize it at the time, but this gave him an opportunity to review the place where the group would spend its last full day in Ghana-Kokrobite.

In the early evening, the majority of the group attended a concert featuring Akilah and Christopher of New York, and William of Kansas, as well as a fashion show, displaying beautiful, hand-crafted wearing apparel. The models were charming and delightful, according to those in attendance. Many in the group decided on outfits that would be purchased later.

The group gave favorable comments about the evening, such as Regina from New York, who stated, "What a beautiful feeling in the coming-together for entertainment in such a wholesome atmosphere" and Constance from Denver, who said, "The music provided by the unrehearsed musicians was fantastic."

This was also the night that the group finally heard from Brother Kwame Ture, formerly Stokely Carmichael, who has lived in Africa (Guinea) since 1967. According to one member who attended the event, although the group commented about the entertainment, it seemed "obvious" early on that there was a "serious lack of political awareness" in the collective psyche of the group. This was "true" [according to this one member] about their knowledge of current events, as well as the historical significance of past African history. This is not a demeaning revelation. In fact, this supposed state of the group's collective consciousness may well have been the main factor contribution to the sheer dynamism it exhibited throughout the trip.

Commented one member who witnessed the speech of Kwame Ture: "I'd be surprised if any member of the group didn't remain in contact with at least several others on the trip. The group's rediscovery of its Africanness was powerful.

"Kwame Ture's speech, in a dimly lit night club, was historically informative, currently relevant, and powerful. If I was forced to critique the planning of any part of the great trip by Akbar Muhammad and his family, I'd say that the speech by Kwame should have been made early in the adventure. Not necessarily in the full context that he gave on this night, but Kwame should have been assigned the job of giving the group an overview, a history of Ghana in particular and of continental Africa in general."

Brother Ture accompanied the group on several excursions. He stated at the beginning of his introduction on our first day in Ghana, "Akbar told me several years ago he was going to move to Ghana. I told him then that if he did make such a move, I would come and help to settle him (Akbar) down. As you can see, he is here and so am I."

The brother Ture's speech impacted significantly on the political understanding of the group. He said that all conscious Africans are working to unite the whole continent. This legacy, from the work of Ture, Nkrumah, DuBois and other great leaders is called **Pan-Africanism**.

The Village of Aburi

The day started, for many, in the usual manner with a light breakfast of coffee, tea, toast, and water providing the nourishment to sustain the excited adventures which turned out to be for them one of the most delightful highlights of the stay in Ghana.

By this time into the adventure, the art of loading the bus, taking a head count, listening to instructions, and adjusting headphones was down to a science. Within a matter of minutes we were off to one of the mountainous sections on the outskirts of Ghana, the Village of Aburi, which is known for its beautiful and unique wood carvings.

The big excursion moved rhythmically up the narrow winding mountain road. The scenic view from the windows was awesome and truly magnificent to behold. Tears filled my eyes, as my imaginative mind drifted back in time to proud landowners who tamed this mighty land and developed great empires that were later stolen from them by foreigners who took advantage of their kindness and friendship. Here we see, once again, another example of how the African people, generous and kind in nature, were exploited, misused, and ultimately forced from their land. The means by which the newcomers acquired the land was treacherous and inhumane. A trip to Africa is bound to awaken the self-identification and value of the legacy stolen from African people. That identification and appreciation for that value is the basic requirement for us, individually and collectively, to methodically develop institutions and systems for the total reclamation and restoration of both the African land mass and its great people.

Near the top, or the end of the upward journey, I could look down into the deep ravine with its layered greenery stretching for miles that left me wordless to express the emotions generated by the beautiful and majestic land. How inspiring and rewarding was the mere sight of the land upon which my ancestors trod, although in their later years it caused them much pain and suffering. Is it any wonder, I thought, that others have returned from Africa with a renewed determination to join the struggle of our people?

The woodcarvers of Aburi are special people. Woodcarving is an art that is hard and time-consuming to master. Consequently, many of the children turn away from woodcarving to easier vocations when possible.

The wood used in carving is also special. There are three different kinds of trees that produce the wood used. The Aburi tree, from which the village takes its name, is used in the making of intricate abstract objects such as coffee tables, lamps and other inanimate designs and pieces that can be viewed by many with each view providing his or her own interpretation of the master's work. Another tree used is the Cedar tree, which is used for making figures. One can find a carved posture of almost any animal, person, or thing. The third tree is the Csxee tree. It is used for making masks of all descriptions and designs. It is also used for certain types of figures.

The members, seemingly realizing that this trip could possibly be the last chance to use their newly acquired skill of bartering and negotiating prices, methodically moved up and down the narrow strip which I labeled "Carver's Row". What a sight to see as individuals, equipped with pockets burning with their new currency, peered into the stalls, wheeling and dealing. It was a joy to witness the enthusiasm of the buyers and to sense the understanding and genuine appreciation of each other.

The time came to leave Carver's Row and head for the buffet table in the National Gardens of Aburi. Here people come from all over the world to converse in these breath-taking gardens and dine in this beautiful open air dining room. We, the Africans, several generations removed, can still truly understand and appreciate this vast and beautiful "Garden of Eden".

The long table was spread with appetizing African cuisine. Among the native dishes were such renown foods such as: Palava Sauce with fish, Joffof Rice, Vegetable Samosa, Meal Samosa, Grilled Chicken African style, Fried Plantain, Boiled Yams, Contambra and special teas as a refresher. Words such as "super", "out of sight", "unusually tasteful", and many others were used to describe the meal.

The scenery in and around the restaurant was breathtaking. Palm trees lined the manicured walkways. The low and picturesque foliage covered the ground while its creeping finger-like vines attached themselves to any inanimate object that would oblige.

We knew it was time to leave our new-found haven because in the distance, the excursion bus beckoned with a mournful sound, as if it dreaded the task of taking us away.

The ride down the mountain side was different from the upward journey. Conversations and expressions of the group told the story of why we had come these thousands of miles only to spend a few precious hours. We would never again fall into the rut of taking our hard fight for freedom, and the sacrifices that Africans, whether in Africa or America, for granted. The beautiful oneness of the people would prevail and would be forever imprinted in our hearts and minds.

The bus turned towards downtown Accra, where, upon arrival, some group members collected tailored suits made to their specifications by the craftsmen earlier in the week, while others scurried off to the Post Office to mail letters and cards. The die-hard shoppers found waiting vendors at the Art Center who gladly relieved them of their cedi's (CD's-the official currency of Ghana).

Some members of the group found it difficult to bring this day to a close. However, sometimes in the wee hours of the next morning, peace, quiet, and tranquility did prevail.

Section Five

16. Hospitality, Akbar Style
17. Ghana Beaches

Hospitality, Akbar Style

Sunday morning anyplace, anywhere, anytime is a special time in my daily living and this Sunday morning in Accra, Ghana at the home of Minister Akbar, his wife Maryam and three of their lovely daughters, highlighted the adventure in several ways, thus making my day. The breakfast consisting of mixed fruits, eggs, homemade cinnamon buns, cheese toast, and assorted hot and cold beverages was delicious as well as wholesome.

The atmosphere was delightful, hospitable, and the informal gathering allowed not only the fellowship of our group, but that of important African-American dignitaries now living in Ghana as well as V.I.P. Ghanaians to come together for comradeship and mutual visions.

We were completely involved in small talk and enjoying each others company when the presence of Akbar's voice perked up our sense of hearing to listen to him as he emphatically reminded us that the struggle by Africans in Africa is linked to the Africans in America through a direct bloodline and it is time to cut out the middle person who has for so long planted, watered and nurtured the seeds of distrust among two segments of the same group of people on two continents.

Sister Samimah, a pleasant and personable daughter of the host and hostess, greeted the group. She expressed her thanks for the cooperation given to her by all members, from the first meeting in Kennedy Airport, New York City, to the present time. She also handed out several fun-loving type certificates that highlighted some of the unique personalities within the group.

Everyone was having a relaxed and wonderful time when guess what? You got it: the vendors appeared on the lawn. No place, not even the living room of a respectable citizen, can escape the hawk-eyes of the business-minded Ghanaians. However, this particular group does its share of making them welcome. We loved doing business with them. It seemed as though the marketplace is a spontaneous happening that appears without a minute's notice. Racks and boxes of beautiful clothes, crafts, and yards of material were soon covering the lawn. Beautiful hand-crafted African dolls dressed in authentic clothes made a big hit with the group.

This kind of marketing is just another way that the Africans show their ingenuity, craft skills and a willingness to provide financial stability to their country. If they have one hand out to receive a donation, they have something in the other hand to give in return.

While the festivities were going on, there was a gathering of a few members of the group working hard to finalize plans for a group that would ensure the continued visitations by Americans. Entrepreneurship through investments and other participatory adventures were also high in their priority list.

After breakfast, last minute basement bargaining, much small talk, and photo sessions, the partially-filled excursion bus headed for an outing at Kokrobite Beach Club.

The itinerary states: lunch at this particular club. Although some group members are eating lunch as they travel, we must fulfill our engagement by having lunch as planned, because we are reminded of a statement by Brother Akbar earlier, "We are a group, abiding by the democratic process, and whatever the majority decides, others must follow." So eat up members, because it is now 11:30 a.m. and we are scheduled to have lunch at 12:00 noon-so be it.

We were fortunate to have the privilege of visiting some of Ghana's most beautiful beaches. The first one was on the beautiful Atlantic shore of Coco Beach, on the outskirts of Accra, also boasting of a fine restaurant with delicious and wholesome food. The thatched roof of the restaurant and the rolling waters of the Atlantic Ocean added interest and excitement to the pleasant atmosphere. The rest, food, and relaxation prepared the group for its next historical stop, which was the DuBois Centre.

The second beach that we visited was the El Mino beach which is part of the El Mino hotel complex. Here we are dined in a pleasant atmosphere of music, coconut trees with colorful tablecloths that added to the enjoyment of the lunchtime fellowship.

After the meal, some of us ventured down to the water's edge where we collected beautiful sea-shells, small rocks, and unusual pieces of driftwood. Some members dipped their toes into the cool water. Going to the beach at this time was a sedative against the horrendous experience of the last four hours. It provided the calming surroundings needed to relieve the tension and frustration that had built up inside because our last stop of that particular day had been the slave castles which had unnerved all of us.

Our third beach visitation came immediately after our farewell breakfast at the home of Akbar Muhammad. We headed for the shores of the Kokrobite Beach for romping and lunch.

Section Six

19. Farewell to Ghana
20. Reflections

Our last group activity of "The Adventure in Ghana" trip took place at the Sun Lodge Hotel, one of the hotels used by the group. This is the same hotel where we had received our orientation to Ghana eight days ago. The main purpose of the meeting was to receive departing instructions for the trip back to New York City.

Throughout the meeting there was much small talk, picture-taking and newly acquired knowledge exchanging. One could also sense a genuine feeling of low-keyed excitement conveying to one another the happiness and rewards of being a part of this historic trip.

At the end of our final group meeting in Ghana, everyone could be found in his/her room finalizing packing and typing up loose ends. Within a matter of a few hours, phones would ring in our respective rooms for the last time.

⌘⌘⌘⌘⌘

It's 4 a.m., the last day, and the final wake-up call penetrates the still dark hotel room of number 11. The time had come to leave Ghana. The first leg of the trip to Kennedy Airport in New York City begins. Soon the big excursion bus will arrive. Package, parcels, and sleepy bodies will fill it and head out for Accra's airport.

Through customs and whatever was necessary, we obliged, and at 9:15 a.m., we were airborne: one last glimpse of the skyline of Accra as the big jet turned westward with its tired, but happy, campers settling in for the long ride home.

Although we had enjoyed, for the most part, our stay in Egypt and Ghana, and got to participate in and observe the morals and customs of African people in their native land, it is good to touch down on American soil. To sum up what had transpired, and for some, had transformed, their thinking about a land as well as a people that seem so far removed from their way of way of life:

The Ghanaians are hospitable and eager for the chance to upgrade their standard of living, improve an antiquated sanitation system, and produce enough food so that everyone may have an adequate diet. Ghana is seeking also to have at least the minimal health care available for its citizens so that they in turn may become a productive, self-sustaining, and independent people. They have the natural minerals, the resources, the land and the human capacity that are the fundamentals needed for developing into a powerful force that will be able to elevate that whole society into a self-sustaining economy.

The one ingredient missing in the formula for greatness and competitiveness in the world market is technology and the skills to use that technology. Hopefully, individuals, as well as investment firms, will realize the potential that West Africa has.

⌘⌘⌘⌘⌘

Many of us discovered gestures and ways of the Ghanaians that are so familiar to us. We realized that these people are truly our people, and that we must strive, through mutual understanding and financial investments, to build a positive future for the Africans in Africa as well as for the Africans in America.

Notes

1. Those interested in distributorship or other information:
Ghana Textile Printing Company
Box 606
Tema, GHANA

2. SOS Children's Village Association
National Coordination
PO Box 166557
Accra, GHANA-North

3. Dr. Ben-Abdallah is now (1993) a professor at the University of Ghana, lecturing in African History and Political Science.

4. Kwame Nkrumah headed the independence movement of Ghana from Britain in the 1950's and was president of Ghana 1960-1966. He developed Ghanaian economy, as well as the educational and health systems. Change brings dissatisfaction, however: Ghana underwent a coup d'etat while Nkrumah was in China, resulting in the overthrow of his government. Ghana's founding Prime Minister (1957-1960) and first president died exiled in Guinea.

5. The Minister of Education
Education Committee
Accra, GHANA

6. Currently running in Washington, DC, as of November 1993, the haunting film SANKOFA is a memorable treatise on precisely this subject : the underdiscussed atrocity of the sale in human beings, erroneously called "African slavery"; these free men and women were given the status of "slave" upon their enslavement on American and Caribbean shores. Twenty years in the making, the film commences with a graphic account of the treatment of captured Africans at the Castles of Cape Coast, Ghana, and unfolds by detailing the similarly inhumane manipulation of the enslaved community in America and the Caribbean. Haile Gerima, the Ethiopian creator of the film, is to be praised and supported both intellectually and financially for addressing this painful and bitter issue and the injustice on the part of those who desire to forget it.

SANKOFA has the support of Dr. Mohammed Ben-Abdallah, Ghana's former Minister of Culture, and Mr. Akbar Muhammad, International Representative of the Nation of Islam, both mentioned in **Oh Africa, My Africa**. The Author commends Mr. Gerima and his staff, and fully supports the film: SANKOFA-Return to your Past.

7. The Nation of Islam unfortunately does not provide Ju'maah prayer services at this time, only opening and closing prayer.

Glossary

- **Art Center**: A large, multi-purpose, partially enclosed section of downtown Accra where vendors display their goods. Here the group members spent happy hours browsing, bartering, and buying, using their newly acquired skills.

- Cannons: Large guns positioned atop the slave castles. They were originally used to discourage piracy on the seas, but were later used to remind the African captives that escaping from their captors was an impossibility.

- Captives: Africans taken from their Motherland by force and sold in America, and other places all over the world. Cargo ships: The ships that transported the African captives to the American shores. The captives were referred to as "cargo".

- CD: Cedi, the official currency of Ghana.

- Chief: The leader of the people of a particular area, the head of various committees that govern the area.

- Confinement room: A small dark and dreary room where captives were left to starve to death.

- Door of no Return: Through this small opening, the captives, one by one, and often in balls strapped around the ankles, were herded onto the waiting cargo ships for destinations unknown.

- Dungeon: The small underground room, void of adequate ventilation, light, and almost all necessities of survival, where family members were separated, and children and the sick received the same treatment.

- Exploitation: The mayor of Ghana referred to this as a means by which non-Africans who do not have an interest in the welfare of the African people misuse power to further their own selfish causes.

- Imagery: A way of creating a perception for the purpose of influencing others. This can be done through clothes, lifestyles, music, dance, and many other means that are appealing to the senses.

- Slave: A human being who is owned by, and totally subject to, the will of another, as by capture, purchase or birth, a word **first** applied to the captives of Slavic origin of southeastern Europe; the status given an African captive once purchased from the auction block in America or the Caribbean.

- Slave Castles: Large complex of buildings in Cape Coast, Ghana, originally used for the British seat of government and military forts to guard the seas against piracy. With the advent of lucrative trading of African captives, the buildings were used as holding stations until ships were available for transport purposes. Other "slave castles" exist throughout Ghana.

Recommended Readings

MESSAGE TO THE BLACKMAN IN AMERICA
The Honorable Elijah Muhammad

MISEDUCATION OF THE NEGRO
Carter G. Woodson

STOLEN LEGACY
George G.M. James

THE DESTRUCTION OF BLACK CIVILIZATION
Chancellor Williams

THE SOS CHILDREN'S VILLAGE
Herman Gmeiner

THE ISIS PAPERS
Frances Cress Welsing

The Library of Cheikh Anta Diop

The Library of J.A. Rogers

The Library of John G. Jackson

BLACK MUSLIMS IN AMERICA
C. Eric Lincoln

A TORCHLIGHT FOR AMERICA
Louis Farrakhan

BACK WHERE WE BELONG
Joseph Eure and James Spady

FORTS AND CASTLES IN GHANA
Albert van Dantz

THE WRETCHED OF THE EARTH (translated from the French)
Frantz Fanon

BLACK SKIN, WHITE MASKS (translated from the French)
Frantz Fanon

THE TRIAL OF J.J. RAWLINGS
Kojo Yankah

THE SUPPRESSION OF THE AFRICAN SLAVE TRADE
W.E.B. DuBois

DOCUMENTS ILLUSTRATIVE OF THE HISTORY OF THE SLAVE TRADE TO AMERICA
Elizabeth Donnan

Nancy H. Sweet Biographical Sketch

Nancy H. Sweet, a free-lance writer and author of the book **Oh Africa, My Africa** is a unique and multi-dimensional person. She has a natural interest and curiosity for the unknown.Consequently, she often becomes involved in stimulating situations which momentarily satisfy her urge to seek out new adventures. Soon, however, the short-lived satisfaction gives way to new frontiers.

At the age of four, she received *The Three Little Pigs* storybook, a birthday present from her mother. Before long she could master the words and was often seen reading it, even upside down (strictly through memorization). That little book was the catalyst that propelled her into the world of travel through the printed page. Even today, a book or some type of reading material is never more than an arm's reach away.

Her (deceased) parents were ordinary people by Western standards, who successfully instilled in their eight children (the eldest died at age five) the value of setting goals and working towards those ends.One of her father's favorite sayings was "If you want something bad enough, all you have to do is get started and don't quit until you have it."

Like many people, Nancy has a hobby, but unlike most, her hobby is attending school, writing difficult research papers, and other activities that many would call "boring". While others are collecting rocks, stamps, shells, turtles, etc., Nancy collects degrees. In addition to her Bachelor of Science degree in Education, she has earned a Master's degree in Elementary Administration and Supervision, a Master's Equivalency in Elementary Education with a concentration in the primary grades, a Principal's Certification (primary through eighth grade), a Lay Minister Certificate from Albright College, a Missionary Certificate through the AME Church, and is presently a student at West Chester University (PA) seeking a Bachelor of Science in nursing; if plans continue on schedule, she should complete her studies in 1994.

She retired after teaching 16 years in the Great Valley school district, Malvern, Pennsylvania, because of an injury suffered on the job and a knee injury suffered years before that decreased her ability to give 100% of herself.

The author firmly believes that reading and writing go hand-in-hand: if you have the love for one, you can readily develop the other if the desire and the necessary commitment are there.

Her writing of **Oh Africa, My Africa** is the end product of her "raw notes" of the "Adventure in Ghana" trip where she volunteered to keep a running log of the group's activities.

Although some situations were painful, the overall trip gave the author insight into some of the whys and whatfors of the beliefs of not only African-Americans but also Americans of the European extraction as well.

One example would be the misnomer "the African slaves"; in reality, these individuals were African captives whose slave status was established on the "Auction blocks" after reaching the American shores. Several other samples are cited.

The main purposes of the book are

- to raise the conscience level of everyone, generally, and to specifically, create an awareness in African-Americans of the conditions which our foreparents-Africans-before and after their abduction and enslavement by the greed-driven captors, endured, and

- to encourage African-Americans to seek the truth through Motherland visitations, research and all other available means which will, in turn, clear their minds and eradicate the devastation of a worthlessness mindset brought on by over three hundred years of falsified information.

⌘⌘⌘⌘⌘

Africa in the 1400's

Many highly organized states existed in Africa long before the European colonial period. This map shows the main states and trade routes of the 1400's.

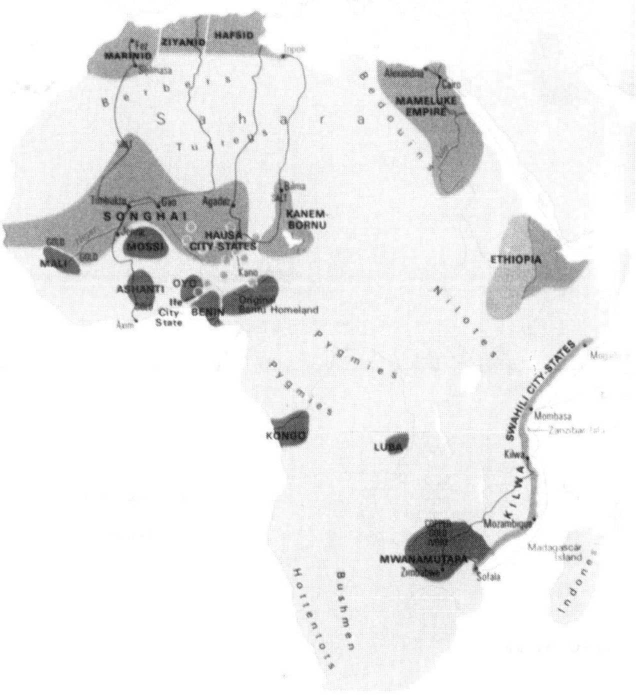

Islamic state

West African state

Bantu state

Christian state

Berbers Major ethnic group

GOLD Important trading product

Land trade route

Sea trade route

0 1,000 Miles

0 1,000 Kilometers

IN LOVING MEMORY
OF MY HUSBAND,
WILLIAM H. SWEET, SR.
WHO PASSED AWAY
ONLY A FEW DAYS BEFORE
THIS BOOK WENT TO PRESS.

AS AN ENGINEER AND
DEDICATED FAMILY MAN,
HIS GREATEST DREAM
WAS TO ESTABLISH A
FAMILY BUSINESS. HE
ACCEPTED DEATH, KNOWING
HIS DREAM IS A REALITY.

PEACE,
NANCY H. SWEET
WIFE